SQUASHING
CHAOS

SQUASHING CHAOS

A PRODUCT MANAGER'S TOOL FOR SETTING
AND COMMUNICATING PRIORITIES

MATT BERNIER

CONTENTS

THANKS

Thank you to my family, who has been there watching me learn everything that I have shared. Learning has not been cheap for me at all. At times, I have been frustrated, exhausted, or just downright surly when things weren't going well. I love you and appreciate you.

Thanks to all of the coworkers who learned these things or dealt with me learning them on the job. I know it wasn't always roses and unicorns, but we did good work and we got a lot done. I couldn't have learned this without you being there calling bullshit and sharing feedback so I could iterate.

Thank you to everyone who helped motivate me to write and helped me to make this book into the presentable form it is in now. I know my writing style is wacky, stressful, and generally poor. I appreciate your expertise and help with getting it where it is today.

Thank you to the reader who actually looked at this book, downloaded, or purchased it. I hope you find it helpful and I appreciate that you spent some time with me and at least being willing to give my book a "no thank you bite."

INTRODUCTION

A HEADS UP ABOUT MY WRITING STYLE...

I don't write documents, books, or whatever the hell this eventually turns into like other people do. I refuse because it isn't me. I want to be me, damnit! I tend to write as I would speak to you if we were 1:1 or if I was doing an in-person training. I write like you're a human who needs to be entertained (or is at least willing to read my writing in a way that entertains me). Yes, I pretty much start by balling up my fists and hammering at the keyboard until I've managed to recreate something akin to the success Shakespeare's Monkeys achieved. Instead, I am the typing monkey who simply vomits his inner dialog onto the page.

Oh! I also like to add random sidebars in the middle of pages and in paragraphs, like the one I'm about to add here:

> ### SIDE NOTE
>
> It's odd to me to type the phrases "write down" and "on the page" because I know that Google Docs and MSFT Word™ Skeuomorphed (is that a verb?) paper into a digital form. Yet, I'm still sitting here in my cold-ass basement typing the words "write down on paper" via a keyboard, and we all accept that as OK. I'm being as direct and honest as I know how to be in this book and this next sentence is an example: To be clear, there's not a single person who wants me to WRITE anything on paper because I can't even read what I wrote

To all the people who are thinking, "He painstakingly went through and drew the sentence diagram for every line of this book." Let's be honest, you know I didn't. I also didn't spend days editing and rethinking the choice of every single word in this document. I did spend many hours convincing myself that I was pondering the value of the sections instead of getting off TikTok or Merge Dragons to go and write this book. I also thought long and hard for .05 seconds about whether I should avoid words like "damn", "shit", "fuck", and other words that entertain me. I decided I don't give a shit because they are just words, and that's how I talk in real life. Deal with it <cool guy pixelated glasses here>. Also, didn't someone do a study that proved that smart people curse more? This means I must be super smart, right?

> ### SIDE NOTE
>
> The Google preview of the link mentions that cursing is correlated with being smarter, but it does not cause people to be smarter. This cracks me up because I am sitting here writing a Product Book and justifying my use of words like "ass" and "fuck" in this purportedly "professional" text, through a correlation that was found in a study. Using correlation is fine for justifying silly shit like cursing in my book but just be careful you use it as a tool that might not always be helpful. Please avoid falling prey to correlation when you're justifying your products, okay?

Fun fact, later on, the article makes a claim that cursing might help with pain tolerance. You're a PM, so might I suggest taking up cursing to make your days a little less painful!!)

WHO AM I?

I am Matt Bernier, a developer who eventually found his way to spending more than a decade in Product Management. It turns out I had a passion for Developer Experience (DX) and the best way I found to spend as much time as possible on DX was to become a Product Manager and influence products as they were built so that Developers were kept in mind.

I had previously taken a detour from working for other people to building a contract web development company with my best friend. We learned a lot, and learning is expensive. At the time, the company was only making enough money to pay me $400 a week and my business partner took home $0 per week. My wife and I were at a stage where we wanted to start our family and that happened rather more rapidly than we expected. We needed more income than the business could possibly bring in. I had to end the business relationship with my friend, which unfortunately also put a long pause on our actual relationship.

I reached out to a buddy from the Denver startup community who was recruiting for technical positions. I don't remember his exact words, but he basically said "I don't have any roles that match your skill set with my clients, but you could come and work for me." So, I ended up working for my friend's recruiting company where I built a recruiting pipeline that resulted in a backlog of candidates our recruiters could reach out to. That role taught me about empathy, integrity, kindness, community, and inadvertently how to find a job I was interested in. I learned which local companies I wanted to work for, due to their reputation, the people who got placed there, and the connections I had to their employees. After two years of recruiting and community building in Denver, I was ready to get back into the startup world. I reached out to a few people I had met along the way, interviewed, and got a role at SendGrid. I got the role I applied for, "Docs Developer" which meant I managed the platform and the content of the documentation. This role turned out to be a great way for me to get back into tech, prove my technical chops, learn the features of the product, and find something I was really interested in going forward - Developer Experience (DX). I was hired into the Developer Relations team, which was 100% focused on how to make SendGrid approachable for developers who needed to add communications to their products. The successes that I saw in my role and that I saw in my team all came down to the idea that the more approachable and easy-to-use the product, the more likely a developer would "put it in their toolbox." We saw developers come back 2 years after they met someone on the team to say "I saw you on stage two years ago, and I just got the opportunity to use SendGrid at my job." This was eye-opening, that the customer experience is part of the adoption funnel for customers, and solidified the importance for me.

I got tired of being asked "Hey Matt, where are the docs for [some product that just went live]" and not knowing what the product was, why we built it, how it worked, or what docs were needed for it. So, I started crashing Product Management planning meetings to stay on top of what was coming and when. At one of these meetings, I helped myself to lunch, since I was already there. One of our Engineering Managers and the Product Manager she worked with closely struck up a conversation and strongly hinted that I should apply for the open API PM role on the Product team. I said "Nah, I'm good" and they hinted stronger. I grabbed my lunch, sat and thought about it, and then walked over to my grandboss who happened to be the hiring manager for the Product team at the time to pitch him on me taking the role. Except that I didn't say I wanted the role, I said that I would be interested in applying for the role if I could modify it to "Developer Experience PM" and add the scope of Docs and SDKs to the API responsibilities. I was told to put together a pitch and present it.

I presented that pitch and I got that job. I then built the Developer Experience team at SendGrid and we went on to build the docs team, release and manage many open source repositories across 7 different languages, as well as aid in the creation of the SendGrid v3 API which at the time was the first time since starting that SendGrid had taken on the idea of versioning the API and releasing breaking changes to features across the whole API. Since SendGrid, I have worked on multiple teams at different companies in technical roles all focused on improving the Developer or Customer Experience.

The constant that I found in these roles was that when I was organized, I was able to be Proactive, with my communications, and my task list, and this led to happier teams, happier coworkers, happier management, and with the extra focus and latitude … better products.

I have spent the last half of my career teaching teams and other Product managers the techniques and approaches to being a Proactive Product Manager but hadn't really put all of my thoughts down in a way that people could use without me being in the room.

This leads me to the book you're reading. The information I have shared here is the result of what I have learned in my attempts to continue to be happier and more productive in my jobs, deliver better products, reduce miscommunications, and build happier teams and bosses. My sincere hope is that you find this information useful and helpful in what you do, whether it's Product Management or something else.

If you do, or you don't, the only way I can provide a better product is if you give me feedback. It is always welcomed and appreciated. You can reach out to me through https://www.mbernier.com and let me know your thoughts, questions, and feedback.

FROM REACTIVE TO PROACTIVE: THE EVOLUTION OF A PRODUCT MANAGER

This might seem familiar and if it does, please understand that this isn't a judgment of you. Being reactive in this role is so common and easy, that it can sneak up on you and take over your whole world until you realize, "Shit, it happened again."

It has happened to me more times than I can count, in jobs where I had things completely organized and got lazy, and in jobs where everything seemed fine but then they weren't. The trick is to find the things that work for you and let them keep working, to not get complacent, and to keep iterating and adapting as you go.

Every job, every team, every product, and every feature will be different and may require some iteration in your approach. What works today will probably not work after the company adds 50, 100, or 500 new people. Being adaptive to the world around you is the number one thing you can do to be a Proactive Product Manager.

SO, WHAT IS A PROACTIVE PRODUCT MANAGER?

Being proactive as a PM is about having small systems, organizational tools, and steps that you take to make sure that you can not only find what you need when you need it, but you are prepared to speak to it and handle questions on it with confidence.

It's about knowing your world, your customers, your team, and your projects without having to keep everything in your head all the time and making sure that you have communicated what's going on and why before people have to ask. Today, that might mean that you have to go out of your way because the way you work is chaotic and stressful.

My goal is to help you identify the sources of those stresses, show you how to look at them from a different angle, share what has worked for me, and hopefully give you the tools, systems, and steps you can take to not only be proactive but to be seen as proactive, and respected for it.

One thing you will see me say in every book and every chance I get, I cannot learn without feedback. So, if you find that something I shared isn't working for you - tell me! If you find it is working - tell me! As a Product Manager and a person who actually really wants to provide a positive helpful product to the people willing to take the time to read, watch, or participate in what I am putting out in the world - I can only make it better with more information about the situations you are dealing with and how it has gone for you. If you have something to share, let me know at https://www.facebook.com/ProactiveProductManager or on my website https://www.mbernier.com.

WHY THIS BOOK: MY PERSONAL JOURNEY WITH ONE OF MY FAVORITE SALES TEAMS

The thread that got me to the idea of the Proactive Product Manager started early in my career whenever I took the time to break free of the reactive situation I was in by stopping work to get organized, set clear expectations about what I was going to do, and then move forward. I have been doing this for years, honing the concepts and tools that I used, and all of this information was sitting in my head ready to pop up whenever the situation arose at work.

The specific situation I am writing about here is the one that led me to start thinking about writing all of this stuff down and sharing it happened much later than I would like to admit. If you were to look at the completion rate for the list of projects that I worked on at this specific job, you would wonder what the hell I was doing there. For the first 6 months, I was asked to pick up a project and then hand it off to someone else. To many people, this would sound awful. But to me, it was wonderful. I was able to have a project long enough to get in, learn about it in the context of the business, get it organized, and hand it to someone else who was either new and I helped onboard them, or they were ready for the next project. I was playing pinch hitter and I loved it.

The hairiest project I picked up was for a team that was building integrations for the company. It was closer to 100 projects all owned by a 6 person engineering team. This team was responsible for a large percentage of the interfaces and code that brought data into the company from customers and sent the data out to 3rd parties. Like most integrations teams on the planet, they were completely overwhelmed by new integration requests, changes at integration partners that required modifications to current integrations, bugs, scalability, and after all team morale. They were getting steamrolled, constantly.

I did some research into the team's backlog, looking at what they were saying they were working on. That part made sense, but the items were not progressing from sprint to sprint. I started getting status update requests as the Sales team, Exec team, and

Support teams found out I was involved. I would look at the backlog and couldn't figure out the status of the projects I was asked about, and they seldom matched what I heard about in the team's standup. I also started to recognize that what was being talked about in standup wasn't matching what was on the board, which explained the whole "tickets aren't moving" phenomenon.

I started recording what the team was working on, both from their current sprint board, their conversations, the requests from internal folks, the customer requests that made it to me directly, and the backlog of things that were noted but not updated. Then, I sat with the team and asked them "Seriously, what are each of you working on right now?"

The answer was that we had something like 20 different things that were Work In Progress (WIP), about 15 of them were considered "nearly complete" by the team, and almost none of them were moving forward at all. We went through each project and discussed the questions the team had, who asked for the work, what the team knew about the impact of their work and these features, as well as what they believed the remaining work would take to complete.

I talked with the team about how the tasks were coming to them, why we should be tracking the tasks, and what they believe the lowest-hanging fruit would be - so they could get a freaking win on the board. We agreed to the things that would be next, based on what we could likely deliver fastest and get off the list, and the team got started. Some of the things they paired on, some they tackled one at a time.

While this was the first iteration of what would become a year's plus worth of work with this team by myself and then by the PM who we hired to work with the team every day, we made initial progress quickly and started to show the team how to get away from being reactive. Within a couple weeks, we were delivering the things that were nearly done and able to get customer and internal feedback. The team was happier because they were knocking items off the list and lowering the cognitive load of having all those projects in their heads.

After the team and I talked and they started working on only the things that could close soon, I started having conversations internally with all the folks who were asking for things. I showed them the list and how it was organized, I asked them for their first thoughts and opinions on how we selected what to work on first, and then I let them know that all new requests needed to go through me for the time being so the team could focus and start delivering against this plan.

The thing that blew me away, still to this day, because I had up to that point never heard a salesperson say it when I told them all the things they wanted that were "mission critical for this deal" or "a blocker for that customer" - was when the Sales team said "Thank you" to me. I had just shown them a huge list of things that were not going to get done any time soon, that were "blockers" for their customers and they thanked me! I took a moment. I was blown away. I thought maybe it was a joke or something, and I just told them "I did not expect that reaction. I fully expected that this was the beginning of weeks of escalations with my bosses, discussions, and litigation of all the details... Seriously, I don't get it, what is happening right now?"

The response I got was "This is the first time we understood the prioritization for this team, why it is the way it is, and the context in which it was made. I can now definitively tell my customers where their request is in the queue, whether it's likely to happen or not, and what they are going to get in the meantime. So, Thank you." OK, my memory is not perfect. I am telling you the "rainbows and unicorns with sparkles" version of this - because

I can't remember the exact words, but damnit the sentiment is the exact same and the words are as close as I can remember, so I hope that's good enough for the purposes of this story at the beginning of this book.

My hope is that I can help you to get your "Thank you for saying no" moment as well. There isn't a promise that it will happen, but I can tell you that using the approach I am sharing here has helped me more often than not to at the very least start the conversations that lead to collaboration, if not the "Thank you."

PART I: REACTIVE PRODUCT MANAGEMENT

I can tell you that every time I have been reactive at work has sucked.

AKA THE PERILS OF SAYING "YES" TO EVERYTHING

"If you stand up for nothing, you'll fall for everything"
— *Alexander Hamilton*

SIDE NOTE

I am not a paid shill for this or any musical, but seriously... have you seen Hamilton? It's good, it's entertaining, and you're learning about some seriously cool history. Even if musicals aren't your thing, watch it at home and have some fun with it!

This quote is not only true in the context of Alex's time and situation, but it is also true for Product Managers who are trying to take control of their backlog and pick the right problems to solve from all of the opportunities that are in front of them. Everyone around you will have an opinion about what should be next and if you don't have one, you will be issued one with a quickness.

How do you justify someone else's opinion? "Oh, well the CEO said we needed to do this, so we should do it" - Yeah, okay, sometimes. But, are you a Product Manager so someone else can hand you a list that you take at face value and implement, all so you can reap the benefits of the absolute disaster that is likely to happen when you don't know why this is even something we should solve? What about when someone comes and says "Why this thing and not this other thing?" How do go about confidently answering that question? "Well, the CEO said so!" Yeah, good luck with that.

If you want to undermine any trust that people have in you as a Product Manager, start with "I am doing this because I was told to" and never have an original thought and don't bother collecting the information that would allow you to confidently speak to the reason why you're spending the company's money on this work and not that work. You'll have a hell of a time moving up in any organization that has a strong Product Management team if you can't find or at least understand real customer problems and motivate your Engineering team to work on them, as well as explain why they are the most important thing to work on to your coworkers and bosses when those questions inevitably come your way.

Not only does authority have the ability to influence you and your team's backlog, but so does the Sales team because if they are worth their salt they are literally building the value of the company one deal at a time. When they focus on enterprise customers, they are doing this in huge leaps and frankly, a $Xmm deal that "makes or breaks our year" can be intimidating when the deal is seemingly on the line for whatever feature they are demanding be written into the contract on whatever timeline. Sometimes, you do these. Sometimes, you say "No, we cannot do that" - You need to know why and be able to justify it because someone high up is going to show up in your calendar mandating a Zoom call on their schedule, not yours, and you should be ready to speak to your answer. Not only that, but in 3 years when you did nothing but build product features for your largest customers and now your user experience is in the toilet because it's a disconnected jumble of 17 versions of the same feature all behind feature flags for different customers. Someone is going to receive the question "How did this happen?"

Don't be the reactive Product Manager, that path leads to ulcers, rage quitting, unhappy teams, and surprise Zoom calls where you litigate decisions that everyone has long since forgotten about.

If you can break the cycle of reactivity you can get to a positive place where the decisions are known, the problems are understood, and you can confidently communicate the reasons for the chosen path forward - life gets a lot easier and everyone is much happier.

PART I SUMMARY

You just read all of Part I and it was like 5, maybe 6 paragraphs. Do you need a summary?

NEXT

How to actually do the thing you're here to do.

PART II: ORGANIZING THE CHAOS

Most of the time, when I was reactive for more than a week, it was because I was disorganized. As soon as I got organized, things started getting a lot easier.

STEP 1: MAKE A DAMN LIST

Yep. I just wrote all that crap above to get you hooked into continuing to read, all so that I could tell you to make a list. Funny, right? Right?

Seriously though, start with a list. It's that simple. And it's that obvious. And it's that annoying.

SIDE NOTE

I'm only a couple lines into this book and I'm making an aside. Not only that, but like 2 paragraphs down, there's another one. I decided I wanted to have fun with writing this book, so I'm going to damnit.

This tip is just too good not to share, deal with it.

Did you know you can go to https://sheets.new and get a new spreadsheet from Google Drive? It works with https://docs.new, https://slides.new, and https://forms.new for their respective document types, too. This alone has saved me whole seconds of clicking around and waiting for pages to load. #winning

If you want to be able to get from reactive to proactive, you have to get organized and if you're overwhelmed it's likely because you have too many things coming your way and you haven't figured out how or what to say no to yet.

SIDE NOTE

A former CPO of mine, who I might add worked at Microsoft for a little bit, told me "Any time you see someone using a spreadsheet, it's a product opportunity."

I really hope that passing this little tidbit along helped someone who read this book identify a problem that needed solving and turned that into a business that let them take home a couple million dollars or more. If it did, I want to know about it so I can go send him an email and let him know I was listening!

In this case, the product that was made for this solution has the name Jira, Trello, Monday, Asana, Todoist, Google Keep, and for the purposes of our exercise here - Google Spreadsheets. Yep, good old spreadsheet time. Again, you're hooked on reading this and my advice is to make a list in a spreadsheet. LOL. Don't hate me, it gets better, but I have to acknowledge the fact that me writing all this down so that I can tell you to make a list in a spreadsheet feels bad and wrong, even knowing where I'm going with this. If I can muddle through writing this, editing it, formatting, publishing, and spending the time and money to share it so that you find it and read it - I hope you can hang on while I ask you to do the ridiculous task of putting your list in a spreadsheet. Some of you might already have this and are thinking "No shit man" - but, as I said a sentence or two ago, hang on for just a little longer, it gets better and it can be really cool what you learn. At least I hope it will be, and if it's not - then let me know (my Facebook and website links are in the Intro).

Okay, back to the list. My suggestion which will get matchy-matchy with later steps, is to **have a column for a very pithy name for the problem** (if you have a problem), **and a notes or description column for everything else that needs to be added**. If this is already in a task tracking tool and you're hating me right now because it's already been entered into a tool, then copy the title and link to the item in the tool. This isn't the important part, this is just the label so you know what you're organizing.

If you're like me, first I am sorry, and second - if this is the first time you've heard the word *pithy* in a while, you're probably thinking about how that is likely some old English smarty pants word. Well, it might be, I have no idea. But, I do know that there is a damn good reason for your problem or project titles being *pithy*. When you use a title that doesn't imply a solution, one that is simple, straightforward, and gets the point across efficiently (unlike this paragraph) then you set yourself up to avoid problems stemming from assumptions in the future. Project titles that imply a solution have a tendency to create all kinds of drama later when you and someone else realize that you have not been talking about the same problem or solution the whole time. You might have even been using the same words and feeling super aligned, too. Bummer dude. That sucks. So, **the simpler and less descriptive a project name is, the better**. To add to that, **the closer you can get to describing the customer problem and not a solution**, the better too.

PART II SUMMARY

To summarize, because I kind of went off the rails there for a bit, you should end this section with a spreadsheet list of pithy project names and/or a notes field with more info.

NEXT

We're going to get into the fun part, where we actually just make up a bunch of data so that we can organize the list and claim that it is prioritized.

I am completely serious. This is absolutely bonkers and it still works, because Cunningham's Law is a real thing.

I will refer you to the story above about the sales team that said: "Thank You". That really happened and I really brought them a list with "data" that was mostly made up. The trick is to do it out in the open by being completely honest about it. They'll think you're joking, and people totally thought I was joking, too. I wasn't.

I started that meeting, and other similar meetings with an opener like this: "I am going to share the list of everything I could find that the team is or could be working on. The list is real, the ranking is arbitrary and mostly made up. I added the data I was able to gather and used nothing but pure assumption for the rest. Yes, I am in fact saying that this is mostly me bullshitting on why these projects are ranked the way they are. That's OK because the order is just there so we have a starting place for this conversation. If you see something you don't agree with, throw a comment in, and let's chat it out, I'm probably wrong about the ranking and that's totally OK."

If you're stressed right now, just hang in with me a little longer. It will all make sense and you'll see why it works here very shortly.

PART III: WHAT IS RICE, OTHER THAN A DELICIOUS STAPLE FOOD, THE WORLD AROUND?

RICE is a prioritization framework that I learned by reading [an article from Intercom](#) a long ass time ago when I was first trying to be a real Product Manager. If you're absolutely done with my shenanigans, follow that link. You'll get everything that I got and possibly more if they updated the article in the last decade. What you'll miss out on is what I have learned from using it, how I present it (except that I let that cat out of the bag in the last chapter's last paragraph), and a link to a spreadsheet I already set up for you so that you can cheat off my sweet spreadsheet skills (which is fine so long as you don't tell people I can spreadsheet, I don't want to be known as that guy).

The name is an acronym, like so many other memorable things in business and life, that holds places for the words Reach, Impact, Confidence, and Effort.

The whole idea presented in the article is that you can use these to rank your projects and identify which ones are likely to have the highest impact on your customers. To an extent, if you can do it perfectly with good data, this is true. You can come up with a true mathematical formula that is fed by real-life data to pick the most impactful next project.

What I have found though, is that while it CAN be a great objective tool to rank your projects, it is also a solid Cunningham-esque tool for catapulting yourself out of reactivity and into proactivity.

THE TL;DR OF THE REMAINING PAGES IN THIS BOOK

- Find the link to the spreadsheet that I hid somewhere down below
- Copy it to your machine (no promises it will work with either the Mac or MSFT spreadsheet apps) or to Google Drive like a sane person
- Take that list you made earlier and copy it in
- Start picking the values for each of Reach, Impact, Confidence, and Effort.
- Once you're done filling in those fields, right-click the big "A" in the first column and "Sort sheet A to Z"

You're done. You have a ranked list, you made it all up like everyone else is doing in "Business", and now you can show off your work like you actually did something valuable.

Heads up: Some people might agree with your list; some won't; and that's exactly where I want you to be. If you keep reading, I'll tell you how to deal with all that. If you don't, good luck, fair well, and have a nice life! It was special and fun for me, I hope it was for you, too.

XOXOXO,

Matt

THE CALCULATION

I wrote the next section and realized it would be super helpful to just give you the formula, especially since you may not have gone to the Intercom article I linked above. Here it is, in all its wonderfully simplisticness. (Yes, that's now a word, because languages are fluid and ever-changing)

$$(Reach * Impact * Confidence) / Effort$$

When I learned this it blew my stupid ignorant mind. It was like the lights turned on. I immediately felt a sense of decreased Ego and self-worth for not coming up with this myself. Then, I got over that shit and started realizing the potential benefits because if I am the one who brings this in as a tool, I get the credit for it whether I came up with it or not. And yes, just like here, I always give credit to the freakin' geniuses who I learned this from. Damnit.

BREAKING DOWN RICE: REACH, IMPACT, CONFIDENCE, AND EFFORT

I'll give you some definitions. They don't match exactly what Intercom said, because I am applying what I have learned from using this tool, I thought we discussed that earlier?

For each of these, you need to decide what they mean for you and then stick to it. As you use each one, you will want to forget what you put down for other items - the comparison of each row (aka project) in the sheet comes later.

REACH

This is typically used in the realm of the positive effects of:

- How many customers will use this?
- How much of our potential TAM could this impact?
- How many coworkers will this touch?
- How many of the deployed servers will be affected by this?

You're trying to come up with an idea of how many of {whatever} this project is good for.

IMPACT

Where reach was how many, this one is "how much":

- How impactful is this to the day-to-day of {customer/coworker/server}
- How much will this improve {feature/activity/experience}
- How likely is this to positively impact the bottom line of the company? Or the customer?

CONFIDENCE

I will often do this one last, just because I like to think about this as:

- How confident are we in the other choices we made for Reach, Impact, and Effort

or my personal favorite:

- How confident are we that we could sit down and do this work right now, with what we know right now?

EFFORT

This is both the sleeper and the item that controls everything. To set this one, I am asking myself "How big do I think this project is from the start to putting it into customer's hands?"

The reason this is the sleeper is because in the formula it's the denominator (there I go with the fancy language again), and therefore it decides the fate of the project. If it's a big effort, the project goes down the list. If it's a small effort, the project goes up the list.

I have added some protips later on, that will help you to handle situations where the effort is fucking everything up. It will, and if you find that section, you'll be armed and ready for what's to come.

THE FIRST TIME I TRIED RICE

This title sounds like something I would say in Project Manager's Anonymous.

<stands up>

Hi, My name is Matt.

<Everyone: Hi, Matt>

The first time I tried RICE, was on a project at SendGrid. We had so many GitHub issues, pull requests, internal feature requests, new feature requests, feature parity requests, and wish list items that we wanted to accomplish on our open-source repos.

<deep breath>

We only had two people who were tasked to do the work within the company,

<long pause for reflection>

so we had to figure out where to start.

We put everything we could find in a spreadsheet, added completely arbitrary ranking values at first, and then as we were able to get access to better data we added it so we could make even better decisions. Everything was going great.

We used this tool to outpace overall company growth in SDK adoption vs. other options by picking the most impactful projects to work on.

<pause for another deep thoughtful breath>

I have been addicted to RICE ever since.

Thank you.

<Everyone: performs thoughtful snaps and claps>

<sits down>

HOW TO USE THE SPREADSHEET

I promised a spreadsheet in the TLDR at the beginning of this section, and now I am going to deliver. This is a 100% free-to-use, copy, and share Template:

My Introductory RICE Framework Template

STEP 1: GET A COPY OF THE TEMPLATE

Click the link to open the Google Sheet I set up for you. If you're logged in to Google Drive, you can click "File" and then "Make a Copy" which will add this to your Google Drive and let you edit it.

STEP 2: COPY IN THE PROJECT LIST I SUGGESTED YOU MAKE EARLIER

This is my hilarious prank on you because you created a new Google Sheet with that list and spent all that time and now I am going to have you copy all of that into a new Google sheet! <evil laughs>. If you want, you can always delete the old spreadsheet so you don't lose your sanity.

STEP 3: ARBITRARILY CHOOSE VALUES FOR RICE

I didn't write "randomly". I wrote "arbitrarily" because I actually want you to try but I want you to be honest with yourself that on at least some of these, you're likely guessing.

Don't get too attached to the values here, they will probably change and should given more data later. That's a really good thing and solidifies you as someone who can take new information and iterate. Managers and Engineers love that shit.

STEP 4: RIGHT-CLICK OR CMD+CLICK THE "A" AT THE TOP OF THE FIRST COLUMN

This will give you a menu, and one of the items should be "Sort sheet from A to Z". This will sort the sheet from 1 to whatever based on the rank column, which I (ok fine, Google) very helpfully calculated for you already. (I did put in the formulas though - SCOREBOARD, Google!).

STEP 5: ADMIRE YOUR WORK, YOU DID A GLORIOUS THING

Look at the list, and see what you did. Be proud of you for a minute.

STEP 6: GET SERIOUS AND QUIT SCREWING AROUND, THIS IS BUSINESS!

It's time to do the hardest work you have done yet, short of reading this trash of a book - ask yourself some tough questions:

- Does the ranking you produced make sense? If not, why not? You now can look at every project in your list in the context of every other project in the list.
- Did your favorite project hit the top of the list? Does it make sense that it did or didn't?
- What project is at the top of the list? Why? Does that make sense?

If you're not sure that something is correct, adjust the values, especially in the context of the other items in the list. Re-sort. Does this look better?

You now have one of the most powerful tools for inspecting the list of things you and your team could work on. Spend some time with it, get to know it, give it a name, and feed it.

If a new project comes along, go to the bottom and add it in, set the values, and re-sort the sheet. Now you can see where that project ends up on the list. Does it make sense? Why or why not?

PART III SUMMARY

You now hold the tool that helped me switch from reactive to proactive in nearly every job I have had since I started working as a Product Manager. With this, you can get your list to the best place it has ever been so far and then you are ready to share it with your team, your coworkers, and your management.

NEXT

Now that you have a ranking, if you just immediately share it and are not ready for the response, you're likely going to wish you had just smashed your hand in the car door rather than read this book. But, never fear, I gotchu, fam.

Employing this tool takes a little bit of effort, sometimes you might have to shuck and jive a little, as well as practice with being wildly incorrect and owning it like a fucking champ. Let's go!

PART IV: HOW TO SHARE WHAT YOU DID AND LOOK AWESOME DOING IT

First, and this is the absolute most important part, do not defend anything about the work you did here and let everyone know that like *Who's Line Is It Anyways* - "The points are made up and they don't matter". Really really.

This whole exercise was to make each project comparable on some sort of fairground, whether it was arbitrary or not. If you did the work above, you have a list of projects that you can look at and compare their "rank" in the context of the rank that other projects have. You can ask yourself all the important questions like "How the hell did that go to the bottom" and "Wow, why is that #5 when this other line is literally 'print money'".

When you look at what you entered for each value of RICE, you can then double-check your assumptions for each item that is in the wrong place or feels wrong, giving you a better idea of the answers. DO THIS BEFORE YOU SHARE THE LIST! Some asshat will ding you for obvious stuff unless you are really good at deflecting things. A good one, that works once as a joke is, to smile at the pointer-outer and say "Oh, I was just making sure you were paying attention" ... then very quickly and clearly fix the item and rerank it right in front of them while you shake your head and laugh at how silly you are.

SETTING UP THE MEETING

If you like horror films and bikeshedding, then go ahead and invite a room full of people the first time you share the list. If you like your sanity, and have some coworkers who you can mostly trust to give you good feedback and information without being assholes, invite one or two of them for an hour-long "feedback and assumption testing" meeting.

Getting the points in the next section can take some practice, which is why I suggest getting this in front of "friendlies" before you show anyone who can dictate the direction of your career or who will just be shitty about everything. It can take knowing the people in the room, as well as tact before and during the meeting, as well as the ability to adjust on the fly without getting defensive or divisive in the conversation.

You have to be agile and nimble here. Practice it with friendlies, and get their information and suggestions. This will help to lower the overall need for ninja-like deflection in later rooms because you can have the points other people would make ahead of time and include them in the notes. It will also give you more confidence because you will know what the response of friendlies was, which will help you have insight into the potential response of the rest of your coworkers and team.

SHARING THE LIST

There are a few important points that can really help, that you should use to set the stage, as it were when you get into the room and kick off the meeting. Using these helps you control the meeting to get what you want out of it. I've numbered and bolded the points below, or set them aside with some sort of formatting once I turned this into an ebook from a Google Doc, and added notes under each one.

1. WE ARE HERE TO COLLABORATE

When I kick off the meeting, whether it's 1 person in the room or 20, I usually start out with a variation of the following, to set the stage that makes sure that the invitees know that this isn't some magical dictate, and in fact is mostly bullshit:

"Once I compiled the list I went item by item and based solely on my gut, I assigned completely arbitrary values to each project based on what I knew at the time. I then sorted it, looked at how the list came out and asked myself if I thought the list felt correct. Where I didn't like how it looked or couldn't agree, I thought about my assumptions and made some minor adjustments until felt right. Having said that, I don't think any of this is factually correct, and based on how difficult it was to fill this out, I am sure that quite a bit is incorrect. I wanted to share the list for your feedback to see if my assumptions were correct or completely wacky."

Telling the truth like this can be difficult, especially when you are used to let's say, "adjusting the truth" to survive in your job. If you can present this in even slightly close to such a way that you make it really clear that you don't honestly believe that this list is anything close to tablets coming down off a mountaintop, law, or correct - you win.

2. I DO NOT FOR ONE SECOND BELIEVE THAT THIS IS ANYWHERE NEAR PERFECT, OR EVEN GOOD.

The values I assigned to these projects are based on what I knew when I added the item to the list, with the context I had. I don't expect it to be 100% correct, but I took a pass and now I want to iterate with you via your feedback.

3. THIS LIST IS HOPEFULLY RANKED TO BE THE HIGHEST ROI BASED ON IMPACT DIVIDED BY TIME TO COMPLETE.

Facts:

- Low impact or high effort makes projects go down the list
- High impact or low effort makes things go up the list
- We have various combinations of these values

I also like to take away the chance for people to get too far into the weeds on this, by first asking, "Let's take a minute to look at the list in its current state, and let me know if you get any *feels* about something being in the wrong place so we can discuss. Make some notes or comments as you go through and we will tackle them together.

4. IT IS A NEAR CERTAINTY THAT I AM MISSING INFORMATION, AND I NEED YOUR HELP TO IDENTIFY THOSE PLACES

This one is straightforward and really just resets the expectation of #2 and #1 above. You're here to collaborate and you don't exclusively drink your own Kool-Aid.

5. IF YOU KNOW OF A PROJECT OR IDEA THAT WE SHOULD DO THAT ISN'T ON THIS LIST, LET'S ADD IT AND SEE WHERE IT ENDS UP!

This one is key, especially for very helpful and very smart people (I wish there was a really good way to make it really clear that was PURE sarcasm), because someone will come up with something that was missed. It might even be pure gold. It also might be ridiculous, like a solution leading the problem, and maybe it shouldn't be on the list at all.

Who cares. Add it anyway.

By doing this, it proves that you're listening and it triples down on the whole "we're here to collaborate" thing. It shows that you care to include their opinion, even if you don't agree or get along with that person.

WHAT DOES IT MEAN TO WIN HERE?

The win here is that you fundamentally change the conversation by getting people to look at the list objectively, even if the reason it has become objective is completely arbitrary. You could use "How many ducks do you give this project" and it would be just as arbitrary, but I guarantee that you can get a room full of muckity-mucks to sit down and debate that "Well, I say, Cleetus! I believe Project X should be 5 ducks, not 4! And, while I'm yellin' Project Y should be 3!" The win isn't in the debate, it is in the information you get out of the debate when you get to reply with "That's great, what am I missing" or simply, "Cool story, bro. Why?"

You just took away so much bikeshedding about the specifics of each individual item on the possible list of things that you and your teams can work on, and you showed them how to objectively compare the projects to each other.

If someone gives you feedback, ask them what they think the values should be and why. Then, write a quick summary in the notes column and put their name next to it. Sometimes, I will get fancy and throw a date next to it, because these types of lists can have a tendency to live a while if you don't have a system to move them to after you rank everything. The date and the name will help give people context about the thinking when that comment was made. Now, you start to build the case for being a "good collaborator" and "team player". You also get to show off all the work you did to try to get this list to be as close to consensus as possible.

OKAY, GREAT INFO. SO... HOW DOES THIS BLOW UP IN MY FACE?

This is a subject I don't see a lot of books add. I guess they all assume their advice is so infallible that it will never go wrong for you if you follow everything faithfully. I am more of a realist and I have seen some shit, so come with me up Shit Mountain and I will show you some things... I am adding a couple scenarios that I have seen or heard about that could happen and suggestions on how to handle them.

All of these assume that you have done the work to let people know that this is an exercise to start a collaborative conversation, put all the projects in the context of each other, and figure out what information you're missing. If you don't do that part, then it might blow up because you didn't set clear expectations.

THE WORST-CASE SCENARIO: THE OLD - "YEAH, NO"

The people you are sharing with might simply reject the entire list, the exercise, or you for doing this work. This can happen for quite a few reasons:

- You're not on the team responsible and your "help" is seen as something other than your job.
- You might be in an abusive relationship with your job. If there is little to no respect in your org, or your team, or if someone has already decided what we're going to work on, how, and when - there's likely no chance that any of your work is going to be seen for the high quality that it is, and they don't deserve you. Think about it, but it might be time to run away

SOMEONE WANTS TO NITPICK EVERY. SINGLE. DAMNED. FIELD.

These people are often known ahead of time because they do this to everyone. The trick is to either give them nothing to nitpick or put them in a situation where nitpicking just isn't a good move - whether they will do it or not. This makes it their decision to be rude.

When you can, you have options here:

1. If the situation is unavoidable, take the information away. Make a new spreadsheet. Copy the rank, title, and notes. Don't bring over ANY of the RICE values or the calculation. Present the new spreadsheet. (Hint: You can copy and paste without the formulas for the rank field, or just recreate it because the title and notes fields will be in order). If you do this, you might get some questions on how you ranked, but you can deflect and say "Let's use the list in its current form to figure out whether we agree with the order these things are in or not, and discuss why not"

2. Get them in early, go through every damned thing with them, and let them do what they are going to do, so they feel heard and included. At least take notes and put their name on them, these folks sometimes have little tidbits of good information to share and it's better to have them earlier than to be surprised by them later.

3. Only add them when you're in a big room of people doing a close-to-final presentation, where you bring in a stacked room of folks who are already on board and *that* person, so they get drowned out by the rest of the room. Plus, other people know and see this person. So, you have a good chance when you have the numbers.

"THIS LIST IS OVERWHELMING"

Yup. No shit. That's the whole point of this exercise. (OK, don't say that, but it is OK to think it. This complainer totally just validated what you were trying to get across and you just won a personal victory - pat your back. Smile a little. Go on, it's OK. - whether it feels like it or not)

But... for the people who are really just not able to even.

I suggest asking them if they agree with the top 10 items. This allows them to see if they think that these are the correct next 10 things you and the team should work on. You can then get their feedback about why they do or don't agree, and you can adjust. You collaborated with someone who is kind of difficult. Well done!

It is less helpful to ask the same about the bottom 10 because that's likely the dregs. However, you can ask them if they have a project in mind that they totally expected to be ranked higher, and why.

THIS [HUGE] PROJECT SHOULD BE HIGHER ON THE LIST BECAUSE IT'S REALLY IMPORTANT™

I LOVE this one because it allows me to put my product operations hat on, do some more collaboration, and don that sweet sweet Project Management cologne I have tucked away in the back of my drawer that I don't always share. (Yes, Project Management is a cologne, don't @ me).

This could be its own whole chapter, and there's a damn good likelihood that I add more on this in later books.

SIDE NOTE

I haven't added one of these side notes in a while and I bet you forgot they were even a thing or you thought you were free of my insidious distractions. <evil laugh>.

I have ideas for two more books, there's a section later about them. I'm mentioning it here to keep the mystery alive, more on that later too. All of this so that I can claim that I'm not being too much of a distraction with this side note that is now the size of the side note I replaced, all so I could get you back to this critical section of the book. It's important and valuable and has saved my ass a bunch of times. Keep reading now, please

---

To get back to the point of this section, you have some opportunities when this question is asked to help the business realize the value of these MegaProjects™ without having to commit to the 85-year (or whatever timeline) vision they represent.

1. Break it up into smaller projects

The short and sweet answer here is a question:

"Awesome, how can we break it up so that it ranks where it should rank?"

You could also get all formal and say something like "Is it only possible for customers to realize the proposed value if we do the entirety of the mega project? Or, are there value-based milestones that we can provide to the customer or the business along the way?"

Usually, the reason it's so large is because it's so complicated, or there are a ton of unknowns, or it's just a ton of freaking work.

Break. It. Up.

Let's be honest, we already knew that breaking up large projects into smaller ones is the right answer. For some reason, humans in these jobs (ME and YOU included, dear reader) just can't figure this out for every project. I can't explain it. It has to be something like a combination of Ego, self-imposed ignorance, greed, and/or some sort of brain parasite that we get from typing on computers and drinking drip coffee.

> ## SIDE NOTE
>
> Let's just pretend like we all have a coffee addiction, like me, so I don't have to admit my problem and work on my problems. Please don't @ me about your tea or mushroom water or protein shake or whatever, I don't want to hear about it

When you break up a larger project into pieces you can change the impact ROI of both the piece you broke off and the piece(s) that remain. By suggesting breaking up the project, you give people permission to think about the project in a way they have or won't think about it while helping your team or company to realize the dream of building projects in an agile way. When you can find the smaller earlier milestones in the project that still provide value, you give the permission to then decide if you actually need to finish MegaProject™, change it, or stop work because it's wacky as hell.

2. Ask: Can we do a smaller investigation/Proof of Concept project to answer some unknowns, first?

What I love about this, is that you are still "breaking it up" because instead of doing all this discovery work during the project, you let them convince themselves to do it early to make it move up the completely arbitrary-ass list you just presented to them.

You're also doing it in a way that gives people permission to not feel like they are missing out on their dream of MegaProject™ while simultaneously asking them to validate that the first couple, or all, of the steps in MegaProject™, are worth it. Rather than running into a project blindly because "shiny project is shiny and I wanna do it", you give them the chance to answer some of the unknowns ahead of time and adjust the values or break up the project, to re-rank it. The people who do this give the list power and authority, because they are willing to do work to earn the top spot. It can be powerful, don't fuck it up, and don't be an asshole about it.

PART IV SUMMARY

Whenever I have used this method, it has gone well for me. I was able to expose information and feelings that other people had, while also helping to get organize and get to collaboration.

There are, however, no guarantees that this process will go perfectly smooth. Some people may be offended that you wrote down all of this information and are presenting back to them. It might make folks uncomfortable, because it has the potential show a lack of their leadership and expose what they know has been going on the whole time. Your job is to be as helpful as you can to show people that you needed this for your sanity, this isn't a recrimination of anyone else, and that you're asking to collaborate on it with them.

NEXT

Now that you have the list and people are talking to you about it, how do you use it?

PART V: WHAT'S NEXT?

THE EXECUTION OF YOUR LIST

You have set the stage as an expert on the priorities of the list and as a Very Organized Person ™. Now, it's yours to fuck it up. No, really. If you didn't read this before you took all those other steps, I hope that it's not too late to help you out in this phase.

It's not as scary as I am making it sound, but this is important.

Ideas are great. They can be inspirational, and motivational, and as a result, they can make bosses, leaders, and teams stand up and want to build the right things. The reality is that **it's the Execution that matters.**

I am a person who has had a million ideas. I have notebooks and lists, physical and digital, of ideas and thoughts and multi-million dollar businesses. The reality is that I didn't execute on any of them and they will likely be tossed in the trash when I next move to a new house, die, or get moved out of my basement office because one of my kids wants a bigger room. None of those ideas are worth shit unless someone picks them up and executes.

Your RICEd list is the same. I have told you as much and suggested you tell everyone else as much. "It's all bullshit." That is if you don't execute.

Once you have the list, you have shopped it around and gotten feedback, and everyone feels pretty good about it. The last suggested step I have for you might be simpler and even more obvious than the first step in this book: **Execute the top item on the list.**

AN UPSELL, FROM ME TO YOU

In the "people who write books and want to teach people cool tips and tricks to make their jobs better as a career without being an asshat about it" industry, we call this the upsell. I even named this section "The Upsell", so it should have been obvious that this was coming.

I guess **if this sentence is here, it's not an upsell because I don't have anything to sell you...yet.** I sure as hell plan to if this isn't a complete fucking flop. In future versions, I will replace this section with information about the other ideas I have for books to share with the world.

I have a RICE list of things I want to write and share, upsell, or even put in a bigger, longer, even more annoying book full of side notes and stupid sentences in parenthesis. I might actually print one of them on real dead trees. One thing I have later in my personal RICE list is an online course. The Effort is much higher than writing the content and publishing it as books, and this is literally me taking my own advice to "Break. It. Up."

The next project on my list is a similar book to this one but about a very simple Product Lifecycle. It's not to tell you what your Product Lifecycle should be, but rather to look at The Execution I mentioned earlier and break that down into its component parts. To make us think about how we do projects, who we bring in, when, and how we execute to make sure we keep our teams, company, and ourselves happy and sane in this frustrating and fulfilling role as a Product Manager. I am a nerd about "how product managers work" (aka Product Operations) and I have accepted that, Now I just ask that you accept me for who I am.

The second is about all of the opportunities that we have as Product Managers to make our lives easier, by doing specific things at specific times during a project. I am being a little cagey here so I don't give too much information before I finish writing it. In case you didn't know, it's the mystery that keeps our love alive.

This is me, setting out my plan for you - I plan to do more, but right now these are just ideas and it's on me to go and execute.

A REAL ASK FROM ME TO YOU - NOT AN UPSELL

If you had a feeling or three about this book, regardless of the feeling. Will you please let me know?

For example, if you thought this book totally sucked and I just wasted your time. First, I am sorry. You know it's true because I down the apology and gave it to you. It sucks that I didn't meet my goal with this book. I do want to know so I can figure out how to make this more useful. Maybe you have a situation I haven't seen or that I have been in and forgot to add - I'll add it in if that helps someone else to find value here.

It is my intention to provide helpful, lighthearted, and useful information that I have learned along the way through my career. Especially when I learned it due to some highly stressful or shitty situation. If I can help one person be a little more successful, save a project, or inspire their team to work on something awesome - then I achieved my goal here. I definitely don't want to waste people's time.

I tell everyone who will listen that I appreciate feedback and I take feedback seriously. I am interested in improving and I hate looking in a mirror, so I lean on other people to share what they see so that I can look at myself from their perspective. I guess, in a way, I approach feedback a little like I approach Product Management. (I am taking this moment to point out that this was a touching heartfelt moment I just shared with you.)

If I helped you solve real problems, or helped you create new ones, or didn't solve a damn thing for you - I want to know. Tell me. Don't be an asshole about it, but please tell me. Let's ideate and figure out if there's a way to improve the product. I'll thank you for constructive feedback in writing in the "Revised Editions" that I release in the future and make sure you get a free digital copy with the ideated iterations employed.

THANK YOU

I had fun writing this book, and sharing my silly asides, and I hope you had fun and learned something too. If I am not having fun or believing that I am helping with projects like this, I can't convince myself to get off my ass and do more. Anxiety, ADHD, and other diagnoses are a real thing, they suck, and they often mean I have to arm wrestle my own self into my chair to focus more often than I'd like to admit.

Knowing that I am helping someone else makes me feel like I did something towards achieving my life goal of having an impact on the world. Thank you for allowing me to work towards my goal via your time and attention.

See you in the next project,

Mattp

www.ingramcontent.com/pod-product-compliance
Lightning Source LLC
Chambersburg PA
CBHW050753290526
45792CB00008B/2164